Taste. Vegetabl...

LOST iN covers, as varie... ...ue in local expression as the recommen... ... our guides.

Our second cookbook brings renowned chefs from all over the world and their recipes to your home once again. This time the cuisiniers have been chosen for outstanding skill in the ways of the vegetable. And because at LOST iN we value choice, the plant-based dishes are not merely aimed at vegetarians, but at all diets. Let these pages inspire you to embrace more plant produce with confidence and creativity.

The ride will take you on a global gourmet tour of unique restaurants in Los Angeles, Berlin, Amsterdam, London, and Istanbul. In keeping with our M.O., we're covering all bases—from street food to fine dining; from the essence of simplicity to orgies of fermentation. Not only will you emerge with cutting-edge ideas for your cuisine, but you'll also share in the atmosphere of our favourite spots. That's why each recipe comes with a curated music playlist.

Celebrate your taste buds, open your ears and eyes, and send your senses on a journey.

Steamed Zucchini with Coriander and Pickled Orange

Simple and Elegant

Lode van Zuylen and Stijn Remi, Lode & Stijn, Berlin

Brotherly Love

There's an almost brotherly bond between Lode van Zuylen and Stijn Remi who run their eponymous restaurant together in Berlin's Kreuzberg neighbourhood.

It might be because their parents run a bakery and restaurant respectively, or because they attended culinary school together and accumulated skills working together in kitchens.

Either way, it seems to have been inevitable that the duo would open their own venture. Lode & Stijn has matched its serendipitous beginnings; a consistently successful local restaurant serving tasting menus much simpler

than those of the fine dining environments where the owners honed their chops.

Dishes never have more than three or four ingredients, allowing the pure flavours of seasonal and regional ingredients to shine through uninterrupted.

Zuylen's homemade sourdough bread, which he developed while working for the popular Sironi bakery in Markthalle Neun, is as close to perfection as possible. The recipe presented here is a simple vegetable medley for the zucchini lovers out there.

Ingredients

A few young zucchinis, they can be differently coloured and shaped
(One zucchini flower per person)
One orange
One potato
Creme fraîche
Coriander seeds
Olive oil
Verjus (or a light reduction of dry white wine)
White wine vinegar
Sugar, salt
Some leaves of nasturtium or mustard greens

Shopping List

Preparation

Orange Marinade & Vinaigrette

1. Peel the skin of an orange with a zester, add it to a small pot of cold water and bring it to a boil. Once it boils, strain and cool in cold water. Repeat this process once more. 2. Make a syrup from 30% Verjus (or a light reduction of dry white wine will do), 30% water, 40% sugar, some coriander seeds, and a pinch of salt. Cook the orange zests once more in the syrup and set aside to cool together. Once the zest has cooled, chop into small squares. Make a vinaigrette of the syrup, using some white wine vinegar and olive oil.

Zucchini cream

1. Chop one zucchini and one potato in thin slices and sweat in a wide pot with some olive oil and a sprinkle of salt until cooked. 2. Put them in a mixer until completely smooth and season to your liking with salt and olive oil. 3. Add a dollop of crème fraîche to give it some freshness.

Steamed zucchini

1. Pick a round, young zucchini and slice it in thin slices. Depending on the size and the number of guests you're cooking for, you might need two. If you take two, it is nice to pick different coloured ones, so they look bright on the plate. 2. Marinate the slices with a spoonful of the syrup, some olive oil, white wine vinegar, and a pinch of salt, and some toasted and crushed coriander seeds. Set aside to marinate for about 3 minutes. 3. Tear some leaves of nasturtium or mustard greens and set aside. Assemble the zucchini rounds in a tower, with some leaves of the greens between slices. Pinch the towers with a toothpick so they will stay together.

Finishing the dish

Put a pot of water with a steamer basket on your stove. Add the zucchini cream to a small pot. We warm purées and crèmes "au bain marie" (in a bowl in a warm water bath). When the zucchini cream is warm, place layered zucchinis (with the toothpick) in the basket. They need about 2 minutes to steam. In the last 30 seconds, add the zucchini flowers.

Playlist

Assembly

Add the zucchini cream, arrange the towers, spoon vinaigrette over zucchini, add the flower, and sprinkle with salt, toasted and crushed coriander seeds.

Beets with Blackberries, Miso and Radish

Unlikely Pairings

Benny Blisto, BAK Restaurant, Amsterdam

Amsterdam

Ethical Cuisine

On the third floor of a repurposed ware-house overlooking the former timber port of Amsterdam's Houthaven, BAK Restaurant has dedicated itself to presenting only the best ingredients from passionate and ethical pro-ducers. In a space of simple wooden furnishing and wide open windows letting in the subtle nautical breeze, Blisto and his team play with ingredients and present them meticulously. The tasting menu changes daily and is com-prised of whatever arrives from the fields, woods and waters of the region, strictly wild,

strictly local and always ethically sourced. Yet simplicity is eschewed through thoughtful and unlikely flavour combinations, that give nature's seasonal bounty a brand new path on your palate. Take the recipe that chef Benny Blisto has shared, a combination of beets, blackberries, miso, and radish, four ingredients that would have never thought to be married on the plate. Best enjoyed with one of the many natural wines from the restaurant's own cellar, or at home with that one good bottle you've been saving up for a special occasion.

Beets with Blackberries, Miso and Radish

»This dish is relatively easy to make at home, looks great and is a nice refreshing start to a meal on a hot summer day.«

Ingredients

Serves 4
200 g (1 1/3 cups) blackberries
30 g (2 tbs) miso paste
30 g (2 tbs) cream butter
500 g (little more than 1 lb.) beetroot
100 ml (1/3 cup + 2 tbs) beet juice
1 red meat radish (pink radish)
Sherry vinegar
Olive oil
Maldon salt
Citrus marigolds or chervil, basil or other
Crushed ice

Shopping List

Preparation

Blackberry miso sauce
Over a medium heat in a frying pan, melt the butter in a frying pan and add 150 g (1 cup) blackberries and the miso paste. Use a spoon to crush the blackberries a little and let simmer for about 5 minutes. The sauce can remain a little coarse and does not have to be completely smooth. Let the sauce cool in the refrigerator.

Beet
Peel the beets and cut into balls with a pommes Parisienne drill/fruit scoop spoon. If you do not have these, cut the beet into equal pieces the size of dice. Cook the beet in the beet juice with a dash of sherry vinegar and a little salt until the balls are al dente. Let the balls cool in the juice in the refrigerator.

Radish
Use Chinese red meat radish (or any variant). Cut the radishes into thin slices.

Assembly
Spoon a few spoons of the blackberry-miso sauce into a bowl and place the beetroot balls on top. Mix the radishes with a little sherry vinegar, salt and olive oil, and place the radish slices between the beet balls. Place slices of the remaining blackberries and top it off with a few leaves and sprigs of the citrus marigolds and a little Maldon salt. (You can of course also use other garnishes such as chervil, basil, etc. instead of the flowers. Place the bowls in deep plates with crushed ice and serve.

Playlist

easy   moderate   challenging
●○○   ●●○   ●●●

Amsterdam

Roasted Beetroot, Pumpkin and Figs

Not Your Ordinary Salad

Derin Arıbas & Kaan Sakarya, Basta! Street Food Bar, Istanbul

Istanbul

Turkish Fast Food Redux

Derin Arıbas and Kaan Sakarya decided to go back to basics when they transformed a 30-square-metre space in Istanbul's Kadıköy neighbourhood into a food bar. The chefs, who were both trained at French culinary institutes and worked at fine dining establishments, took on Turkey's street food staples, often ignored and too often served with dubious ingredients, and brought them to a gourmet level. The classic dürüm wrap, for example, was filled with slow cooked lamb belly, harissa, yoghurt from Konya, grilled onions, and fresh herbs. And soon the bar itself filled with the curious who wanted to rediscover what Turkish fast food could be when reinterpreted with quality ingredients and fine dining skills. For this recipe, the duo shares the eatery's daily and seasonally changing salad, a favourite lunchtime staple among Kadıköy's working crowd.

Salad of Roasted Beetroot, Pumpkin and Fig   ● ○ ○

Ingredients

Serves 2
1 medium beetroot
1 pumpkin
3 tablespoons (15 g) of cooked black eyed peas
100 g (3 1/3 cups) spinach leaves
50 g (1 3/4 cup) sorrel leaves
2 fresh figs
1 lemon
A clove of garlic
125 ml olive oil
Chopped herbs to your liking, like parsley, mint, coriander, spring onions

Shopping List

Preparation

1. Preheat the oven to 190°C / 340°F
2. Thinly slice the pumpkin, season with olive oil, salt, and pepper. Lay the slices on a baking sheet and bake 8–10 minutes until tender but slightly firm. Let cool.
3. Roast the beetroot at the same temperature with the skin on, until tender. It can take 30–40 minutes. Let cool, peel, and cut into cubes.
4. Finely chop the green herbs.
5. Make a lemon vinaigrette with the juice of a lemon, a good pinch of salt, 125 ml olive oil and a clove of grated garlic.
6. In a big salad bowl combine the cooled vegetables, black eyed peas, chopped herbs, spinach, and sorrel leaves. Dress generously with half of the lemon vinaigrette, season if necessary. Serve with sliced figs on top.

Playlist

15

Home Cooking

Shabnam Syed, Mama Shabz, Berlin

Mother Pakistan

Among the graffiti-bedecked old façades of Reichenberger Str. in Berlin's Kreuzberg, Mama Shabz's bright pink and seafoam green existence fits in rather perfectly. Inside, a steady stream of people order their daily serving of homemade Pakistani food for lunch, happily occupying themselves with Punjabi Pakora Kadhi, Chicken Qorma "Desi Style," or just a samosa with homemade chutneys. A former social worker, born and raised in London with Pakistani roots, Shabnam Syed came to Berlin to bring an authentic South Asian kitchen to the starved capital. Inspired by her mother's home cooking, the self-taught chef started with pop-ups at street food festivals, the success of which paved the way to her very own restaurant. A stark declaration of defiance against the stereotypical curry houses, Mama Shabz proudly celebrates the wide spectrum of spices, flavours and colours of true South Asian cuisine. For this recipe, Syed sheds light on a vegetable ignored by many: okra.

Bindiya (Okra Masala)

»I personally think okra is one of the most underrated vegetables out there. It's incredibly delicious, unique in flavour, and a staple vegetarian Pakistani dish that everyone loves.«

Ingredients

Serves 2
400 g (0.9 lbs) fresh okra
1/2 cup of oil
1 small onion
3 cloves of garlic
8 g (2 tsp) fresh ginger
250 g (0.5 lbs) fresh tomato
1.5 teaspoon salt
1.5 teaspoon of chilli powder (extra hot)
1.5 teaspoon of turmeric powder
2 teaspoon coriander powder
2 teaspoon cumin powder
A sprig of fresh coriander

Shopping List

Preparation

1. Wash and cut the ends of the okra for disposal and then cut each okra in half.
2. Fry the okra in a non-stick pan on a medium heat with a splash of water. Stir constantly until the "slime" of the okra has gone away. Add more splashes of water if the okra starts to stick. Once that's done, set the okra aside.
3. In a new pan heat up the oil. Once the oil is slightly heated, add sliced onions and fry until translucent. Add minced garlic and ginger and stir in. Add fresh tomato cut in quarters and a splash of water to prevent from burning, lower the heat, and leave with lid on until the tomatoes are soft.
4. When the tomatoes are soft, mash them up a bit so you have somewhat of a tomato sauce. Add salt and spices and stir in well. There you have your "masala". Add the okra into the mix with a splash of water and stir in. Let simmer on a low heat for 10 to 15 minutes. The okra should be a little al dente. Let it simmer for another 5 minutes with lid off on a low heat to let the sauce reduce. Chop the fresh coriander and sprinkle to garnish.

Playlist

BERLiN

Celeriac, Rice Koji Crumble and Winter Truffle

Dual Heritage

Edoardo Pellicano, Mãos, London

Michelin-starred Supper Club

Above the experimental fashion store Blue Mountain School in London's arty Shoreditch, a simple dining room invites nine people to experience an innovative culinary experience every evening. Awarded a Michelin star just 18 months after opening, Mãos is like a high-end dinner party, an intimate supper club, where guests are connected by a mutual love and fascination for food. Head chef Edoardo Pellicano sends out one immaculate dish after the other from the kitchen, composed of carefully chosen ingredients sourced from his own farmer in Cambridge. All the things that possess the determination to grow and flourish in the rather cold UK soil land on the plate, reinterpreted creatively by a chef who revels in his Asian and Italian heritage. For this shared recipe, Pellicano has chosen something comforting, a bit challenging, and thoroughly unique.

You built your career working at Michelin-starred restaurants such as Portland and Noma. How did this shape how you cook in your own kitchen at Mãos?

In the early stages of my career I spent a lot of time working in restaurants with creative and unusual menus, building up my experience of flavour and ingredients. After a few years I went to do a training at Noma. The creative process and dedication to sourcing only the best ingredients available was truly amazing to see and I learnt a lot from my time there. However, when I'd finished at Noma I wanted to change my style and cook something different, focusing much more on wholesome food. What I wanted to serve was a mixture of the two, innovative flavours but with a good dose of comfort that comes with more familiar dishes.

You're Italian and Singaporean and it was your father's Italian restaurant Ibla that inspired you to become a chef. What made you decide to

focus on Asian flavours and techniques rather than Italian in your own style?

I grew up eating Asian food and flavours—even my dad cooked Asian food at home. For me the connection is stronger with Asian flavours and techniques because that's what we used to eat at home. I can be more creative with Asian flavours, the spectrum of ingredients and what we can do with them is broader. Having said that, I'm still very much fascinated by the ancient cooking traditions which you find throughout Italian culinary heritage.

What preliminary tips would you give home cooks interested in experimenting with new flavours and ingredients and widening their knowledge of food?

Don't ever be afraid to try new things, it might not always work out, but the more you try, the more you can understand the flavour combinations that work. Trust your instincts and never ever stop tasting.

Celeriac, Rice Koji Crumble and Winter Truffle

»I wanted to make a celeriac tart in the same sort of spirit as a classic tarte Tatin, to give that incredible caramelised dessert we all know and love but with a different flavour combination. I also wanted to introduce rice koji crumble because it gives that extra layer of flavour and texture which also caramelises really nicely.«

| Ingredients |

Celeriac tart
3 Granny Smith apples
2 kg (4.4 lbs.) celeriac
30 g (2.11 tbs) cold brown butter
180 g (ca. 3/4 cup) brown sugar

Crumble
112 g (3/4 cup plus 2 tbs) dried rice koji powder
112 g (3/4 cup plus 2 tbs) sugar
94 g (3/4 cup) oats
56 g (1/2 cup) flour
94 g (6½ tbs) cold butter, diced

Shopping List

To serve
Winter truffle × 20 g
Acidic sour jam of choice

| Preparation |

1. Thinly slice the celeriac and apple with a Japanese mandolin or finely slice by hand.
2. Melt the brown butter and brown sugar.
(To make brown butter—heat a thick-bottomed skillet on medium-low heat. Add the butter and let it melt until the foam turns brown and sinks to the bottom of the pan.)
3. In a large bowl, put all the crumble ingredients together and add diced cold butter. With your fingers, rub together the cold butter and dry ingredients to form crumble like big grains of sand. Store the crumble in the fridge until ready to use.
4. Preheat oven 180°C/360°F.
5. In a round baking tray carefully layer the slices of apple and then brush with the sugar, do the same for the celeriac, alternating layers of apples and celeriac.
6. When the tart is formed, bake it with the lid on for 15 minutes.
7. Take the lid off and cook for another 15 minutes.
Check the tart by poking a knife through the celeriac—it should slide through without resistance.
8. Once the tart is cooked, let it cool and put in the fridge. If possible, put another saucepan on top to weigh the tart down.
9. After the tart is chilled sprinkle the prepared crumble on top and put back in the oven at 180°C/360°F degrees for 15 mins.

Playlist

Assembly
Cut into slices, and shave truffle on top, and serve with acidic sour jam and crème fraîche.

Blind Date

Guillaume de Beer, Breda, Amsterdam

Brabant Refinement

Named after their native city of Breda in the south of the Netherlands, Freek van Noortwijk and Guillaume de Beer's second restaurant opened in 2015 to give cuisine from the Brabant region some refined enlightenment. At lunch or dinner, the restaurant's surprise tasting menus are much like a blind date, asking for trust and a venturesome spirit. Take the plunge to be rewarded with a edible exhibition of originality and skill. Dishes such as mackerel with oyster cream, shiso oil and pickled shallot, or slow-roast, free-range Dutch chicken with Maitake mushroom and grated winter truffle, are deceptively simple yet memorable. It all hinges on Chef de Beer's handling of sustainable ingredients, meaning his creative dishes adhere to a delicate balance. Here, he shares a simple dish featuring the humble potato. Even if you can't get specially grown Maris Piper potatoes, the recipe can bring even your ordinary spud to a new level of succulence.

Maris Pipers with Shallot and "Butter en Eek"   ● ● ○

»I chose this recipe because it's so simple and delicious but the ingredients are so humble. The Maris Piper potatoes are specially grown for us in the Netherlands (in Medemblik), which we combine with our own version of the Volendam fish sauce butter en eek.«

Ingredients

Serves 4
Potato
500 g (ca.1 lb) Dutch Maris Pipers (or similiar potatos) of the same size
1 kg (4 1/3 cup) salted butter

Butter en eek
300 ml (1 1/4 cups) gastrique
Gastrique is caramelised sugar, deglazed with vinegar or other sour liquids, and used as a sweet and sour flavoring for sauces.
300 ml (1 1/4 cups) fish stock
300 ml (1 1/4 cups) whipped cream
300 g (1 1/3 cup) butter
10 g (2 1/2 tps) dashi powder
1 tablespoon (8 g) of powdered sugar

Shopping List

2 banana shallots
25 ml tosa dashi vinegar

Finish
A small bunch of chives

Preparation

Potato
1. Rinse the unpeeled potatoes, dry them and poke some holes around them with a wooden skewer.
2. Melt the salted butter in a saucepan and add the potatoes. Preserve them, depending on size, for an hour on low heat (approx. 80°C). This can also take a little longer. Drain and save the butter for another time if necessary. Let the potatoes cool and cut them into 1½ cm thick slices.

Butter en eek
1. Make this butter sauce while preserving the potatoes. To do this, reduce the gastrique, fish stock and whipped cream by half. Add the butter, dashi powder and icing sugar and mix with a hand blender to a thick sauce. Season with salt if necessary.
2. Just before serving, froth the sauce with the hand blender or whipped cream syringe. If you want to, serve the sauce from the whipped cream syringe. Let it cool slightly before filling the whipped cream syringe with it. Depending on the size, add one or two cartridges. If you don't want to do that, you can also froth the sauce with a hand mixer.
3. Gastrique: In small saucepan add 200 g (1 cup) of sugar and 60 ml (¼ cup) water. Bring it to a boil over medium high heat and let it cook until it turns brown and caramelised, stirring occasionally. Slowly add about 60ml (¼ cup) vinegar and stir until the mixture is well incorporated and check flavour. Take off the heat let the gastrique cool itself down. Step back from the stove to be careful of strong vinegar fumes.

Garnish
Cut the shallots on the mandolin lengthwise as thinly as possible. Leave the end whole so that the skirts of the shallot don't come off. Marinate the slices for at least 10 minutes in the tosa dashi vinegar.

Finish
Finely chop the chives and keep them separate.
Warm the slices of potato gently in and spoon the salted butter without colouring.

Playlist

Assembly
Take four deep small plates or low bowls, divide 3 slices of potato per deep plate and pipe or spoon the sauce generously over it. Finish the dish with some slices of shallot and finely chopped chives.

Amsterdam

NO
SERVI
BREAK

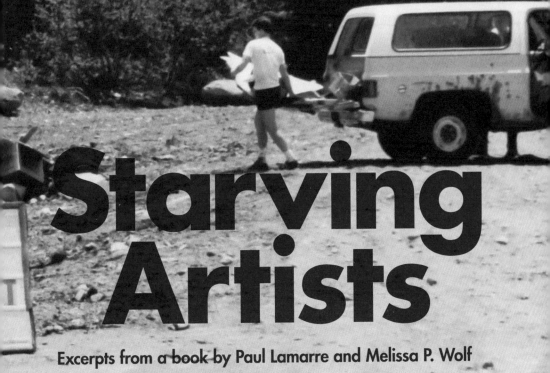

Starving Artists

Excerpts from a book by Paul Lamarre and Melissa P. Wolf

In the early 1990s, US artists Paul Lamarre and Melissa P. Wolf, also known as the duo EIDIA ("Everything I Do Is Art"), collected recipes from a wide range of artists and personalities from the scene. The result was the infamous cook book "Food Sex Art". With recipes such as "Chicken and Pepsi Cola", "Flashlight Jello," and "Boiled Water," they forever redefined the notion of the starving artist

Conversation; with potatoe,
wine, and Brussel sprout...
TM

BEEF

PRO

CUT BEEF

David Jowett Greaves Oxtaby, 1988

EATING MEATballs
WITH green
sauce CP 3/3/87

Benjamin &H.

Gilbert and George, Untitled, 1988

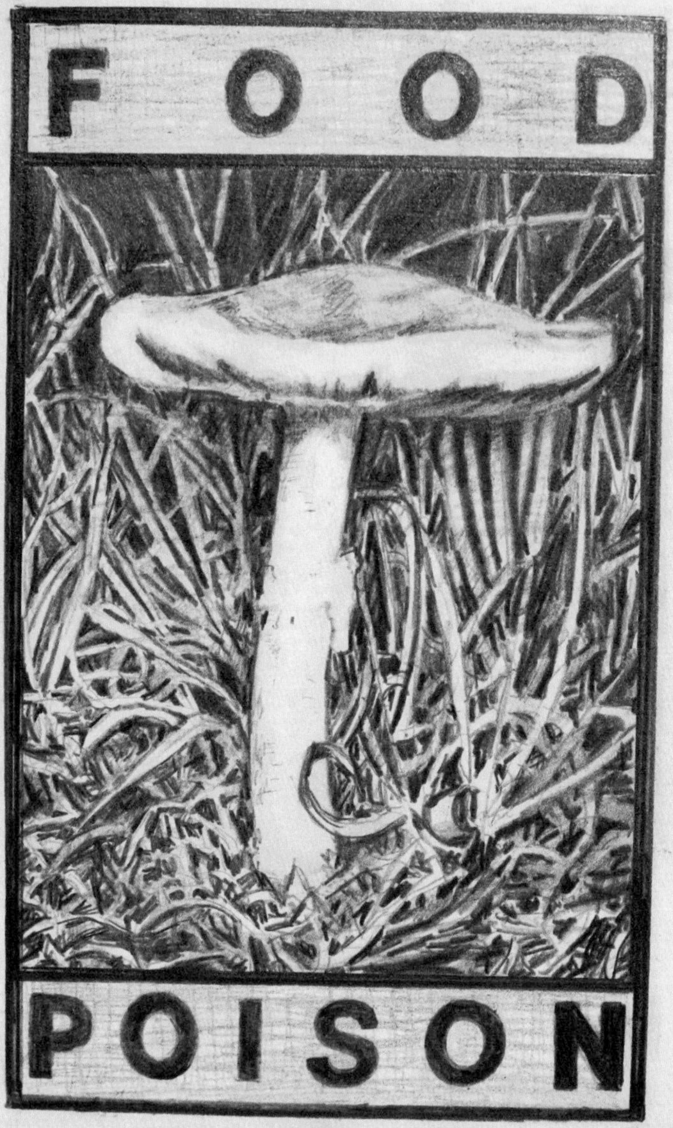
FOOD
POISON

JOHN CAGE, BORN SEPTEMBER 5,
1912, STILL COOKING

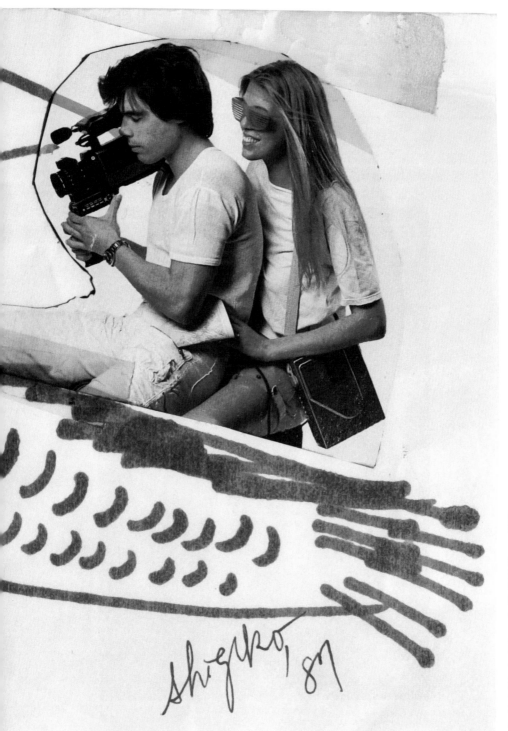

Sashimi: Shigeko Kubota, Sashimi T.V. Dinner, 1987

Endive Ceps

Fermentation
Generation

Michael van der Kroft, Tres Restaurant, Rotterdam

The Cave of Unique Flavours

At Tres it's all about personal stories. From the farmers who have lovingly sown, grown, and harvested the produce that ends up on the plate, to the fishers and foragers who have brought the best of the sea and land to the kitchen. Chef Michael van der Kroft loves to show off all the beautiful things that can be sourced from his country, and he also loves to get a bit complex when it comes to his flavours. Fermentation and maturation are a common technique the chef likes to experiment with, as well as making everything himself, whether it's homemade seasonings, garum or miso. Like a mad scientist he heats ingredients at high temperatures for long periods of time, exploring the unfurling elements of taste. Guests who take the stairs down to his romantic cave-like space, formerly a jazz club, are rewarded with a culinary journey full of stories and thrilling discoveries. With this recipe, the chef challenges home cooks to try their own hands at fermentation.

Endive Ceps

»*This recipe shows the best produce of our suppliers Farmer Perry and Landzicht Biologisch. They grow these amazing kale plants that we pick once a week. We're so lucky we can just go onto the land and pick out what we want. When we saw those kale varieties we decided then and there we definitely had to work with them. This dish was inspired by beautiful kale plants.*«

| Ingredients |

Serves 4–6
Ceps seaweed sauce
80 g (3/4 cup plus 2 tbs) lacto koji
60 g (1/4 cup) yeast broth
25 g (1 oz). dried ceps
1 g (0.04 oz) dried seaweed
6 g (2 tsp) black pepper
2 g (1 tsp) mustard seed
50 g (1/4 cup) butter
20 g (1 1/2 tbs) brown butter

Lacto koji
750 g (1.6 lbs) koji
1500 g (6 1/3 cups) water
45 g (2 1/2 tbs) salt

Chicory
500 g (1.1 lbs) chicory/endive
80 g (1/3 cup) butter at room temperature
80 g (1/3 cup) white wine
12 g (2 tsp) salt
5 g (2 heaped tsp) ground black pepper
0.55 g (1/2 tsp) rosemary
0.7 g (3/4 tsp) thyme

Shallot crème
300 g (10.60 oz) shallot
25 g (2 2/3 tbs) white wine
50 g (1/4 cup) cream
1 tablespoon of sour cream
Sunflower oil

Finish and garnish
Savoy kale leaves
Red kale leaves
Kale leaves
Cavolo Nero leaves
Brown butter
Miso paste
Apple cider vinegar
Raw sunflower seeds
Pinecone syrup or substitute with maple syrup

Shopping List

Rotterdam

Ceps seaweed sauce
Bring ingredients to a boil, take off the heat and let it stand for 10 minutes. Pass through a sieve and only keep the liquid. Blend the sauce with a hand mixer or blender. Put aside until ready to use.

Lacto koji
Blend all ingredients together and let ferment for 5–6 days. Please keep in mind when you choose containers or a ziploc bag to store the mixture, that the fermentation of lacto koji will produce gas. You might want to let the gas out a couple times.

Butter sauce
In a saucepan, bring white wine, butter, rosemary, thyme, salt, and ground black pepper to a boil, lower the heat, and simmer for few minutes. Pass through a sieve and let it cool to room temperature.

Chicory/endive
1. Preheat oven to 80°C / 195°F
2. With a vacuum machine, put chicory/endives in a plastic bag, add butter sauce then vacuum and seal it. Put the package in the oven for 21 minutes.
3. If you do not have a vacuum machine, you can do it in a pot with tight lid. The steaming time can vary so make sure you don't overcook it.

Caramelise
1. In a pan over medium heat, place the vacuum-steamed chicory/endives to caramelise on one side. Set aside.
2. In a pan over medium heat, caramelise the onion with some drops of sunflower oil, stir occasionally until it is nice and brown, and caramelised. Deglaze the pan with the wine and reduce, then add the cream and reduce again. Let it cool down a bit.
Blitz in the thermomixer or blend until smooth.

Finish and garnish
1. Clean and dry all kale leaves. Remove tough stems in the center with sharp knife.
2. Grill the following ingredients on a barbecue grill or grill pan on the stove:
Savoy kale brushed with brown butter
Red kale brushed with miso
Kale brushed with apple vinegar
Cavolo Nero brushed with brown butter

Playlist

Assembly
In each individual bowl, spoon a little of the shallot crème at the bottom of the dish, place the chicory/endive on top and cover with the barbecued kale. Sprinkle some sunflower seeds on top and drizzle pine cone syrup or maple syrup on the kale. Pour the cep sauce on top to finish the dish.

Gnocchi with Broccolini and Green Peas

Buttery Goodness

Basil Gieldon, La Côte, Berlin

Club Med

Getting noticed can be quite the task among the trendy bars and restaurants scattered around Berlin's way-too-cool-these-days Neukölln. One kitchen with true staying power however, embodying the new neighbourhood eatery, is La Côte, where one taste of the small but thoughtful menu is enough to inspire many more visits, with or without reservations. Swedish duo Rebecca Gulam and Felix Bergman opened doors in February 2020, filling local mouths with the sun-spattered fare of Southern Europe and a continental wine list, plus a solid lineup of cocktails at its own terrace bar. In the kitchen, Basil Gieldon sprinkles his stardust with intriguing flavour combinations, having already made a name for himself as chef at Industry Standard and the sadly departed Wild Things. Think of steak tartare with oyster mayonnaise or burrata with peach, basil and hazelnut, partnered by that perfect bottle of wine from somewhere, presumably, Mediterranean and warm.

Gnocchi with Broccolini and Green Peas

»This is a simple but great way of eating gnocchi. We were trying out different sauces for the dish and realised that the more ingredients we added, the more we were taking away focus from the actual dumplings. The focus is on the texture and flavour of the gnocchi and cheese.«

Ingredients

Serves 2
Gnocchi
340 g or 1 large potato, a floury variety
12 g (a little less than 2 1/2 tbsp) grated parmesan cheese
Half an egg, beaten
65 g (1/2 cup) flour type 00
A pinch of grated nutmeg
Salt and black pepper

Sauce
125 g (1/2 cup) cold butter, cut into cubes
25 g (a little more than 1 1/2 tbs) water

Shopping List

60 g (0.130 lb) broccolini
40 g (1/3 cup) green peas
Zest of 1 lemon
5 g (1 tsp) fresh thyme
1 clove of wild garlic, crushed
Salt, Maldon salt

49

Gnocchi

1. Boil the potatoes in salted water with their skins on, then peel them and pass them through a potato ricer. Let it steam out or cool for about five minutes.
2. Add the remaining ingredients and knead the dough on a floured surface until the ingredients incorporate and the dough is soft and smooth—do not overwork the dough, otherwise you'll have tough gnocchi. Rest the dough for a minute.
3. Cut the dough into four pieces and roll into a long rope about 12 mm in diameter. With a floured knife, cut the rope crosswise into 12 mm pieces. Drop the gnocchi into a pot of simmering, salted water and cook until the gnocchi float to the top. Gently move the cooked gnocchi to a bowl of ice water to stop the cooking process. Once cooled, dry the gnocchi on some kitchen paper and set aside.

Sauce

Start by heating up the water in a small saucepan. Once it's about to simmer, add the cold butter cubes one by one, while whisking, to emulsify. Make sure not to boil the sauce or it will split. If the sauce is too runny, simply add more butter. Season with salt.

Blanching vegetables

In a pot over medium heat add water and season well with salt. Once the water is boiling, cook the broccolini and green peas separately. The peas might need a minute to cook and the broccolini only needs about 30 seconds. Drop the vegetables into a bowl of ice water to stop the cooking process, take them out to dry, and set aside.

To finish the dish

Heat up a non-stick pan and add a bit of olive oil, then a knob of butter. When the butter has melted, add the gnocchi. Fry the gnocchi on one side for about a minute, then add the crushed wild garlic and thyme. When the gnocchi are getting nice and golden brown, turn them and continue to cook on the other side. When the gnocchi are done, add the broccolini and peas to the pan to warm them up. Season with Maldon salt.

Playlist

Assembly

Spread the gnocchi and vegetables out on a hot plate. Pour about two tablespoons of the butter sauce over the gnocchi, then grate some parmesan cheese over the dish. Finish with a tiny bit of lemon zest and freshly ground black pepper.

Garden Salad

From Soil to Serving

Dylan Watson-Brawn, Ernst, Berlin

The Unpretentious Frontrunner

What can be said about Ernst that hasn't been said before? Its chef, the too-young-for-so-many-accomplishments-already Dylan Watson-Brawn (pictured left) acquired a very unique set of skills in the kitchen of Tokyo's legendary Michelin starred restaurant Ryugin. It was a feat to become the first "gaijin" (foreigner) in such a kitchen and definitely another feat to open his own restaurant in a neighbourhood that's still a bit on the run-down end of Berlin. But perhaps this was done on purpose, because despite its own Michelin star and its mysterious exterior, Ernst is modest and unpretentious in its philosophy and execution. It's all about the cooking and nothing else.

Tasting menus are long and focus on single ingredients that taste more alive and complex than any normal palate could have ever anticipated. Ernst's brief hiatus on a farm outside the city is just more evidence to the fact that Watson-Brawn is fascinated by his ingredients, and cares about what ends up in his kitchen, patiently following its route from soil to serving plate. The newly renovated restaurant reopened in October and getting a reservation is still something that needs to be planned way in advance. His shared recipe is, as expected, a simple salad with Japanese touches that celebrates the season's natural flavours.

BERLiN

Garden Salad

»Due to the pandemic situation in 2020 we decided to spend some time out of the city building a garden where we cooked outside and only on fire for guests who made the journey. One thing we of course had to serve was a garden salad.«

Ingredients

Lettuce
Batavia Blonde de Paris lettuce
Marvel of Four Seasons lettuce
Chioggia beets (or candy stripe beet)
Ground cherries (or physalis)
Edamame, steam for 5–10 minutes or boil for 5 minutes
Yard long beans
Chrysanthemums (or shungiku leaves)
Itachi cucumbers (or White Asian cucumbers)
Red shiso (or red perilla)
Nasturtium leaves
Zucchini flowers
Basil
Bronze fennel (or young fennel leaf)
Lemon agastache (or lemon balm)
Bean flowers, Chianti sunflowers, Marigolds (or edible flowers)

Dressing
Dashi
Vinegar
Soy sauce
Olive oil
Fig wood infused oil (may substitute with oil of your preference)
Mirin
Kudzu (or potato starch)

Shopping List

Preparation

1. Bring dashi to a simmer and slowly add kudzu slurry (mixture of 1 teaspoon of kudzu 1 or 2 tablespoons of water or broth, and then it can be mixed or heated), and cook for ca. 1–2 minutes until the liquid just coats the back of a spoon. Pass through sieve and chill.
2. When cold, add the other ingredients to taste, according to your preference. Tear salad leaves down to manageable sizes. Toss with dressing and salt.
3. Slice and salt beets and cucumbers. Macerate yard long beans in olive oil and salt.
4. Assemble remaining ingredients on, in and around the salad. Finish with salt and a bit more dressing over top.

Playlist

Frisée, Crispy Potato, Champagne Vinaigrette, Egg Yolk Bonito

Sophisticated Classics

Douglas Rankin, Bar Restaurant, Los Angeles

You're pretty experimental when it comes to your dishes. Tell us a bit about the process behind those original flavour combinations.

It's simple and complicated at the same time. Sometimes they come from an emotion or from experiences I've had that I try to interpret through food. Sometimes it's just me taking risks and putting things together that have always sounded good to me. Other times I use taste to guide me. To be clear there's lots of trial and error involved and it doesn't always work out, but going through that process teaches me more than playing it safe. The mission when we create a dish is always to find something new and interesting that reads simple and uses the least amount of elements. The element of surprise in a dish is also highly underrated and we try to use it to our advantage as much as possible. All that being said, it has to taste great and be something that we'd be very happy with if we ordered it in a restaurant. We cook for ourselves as much as our patrons. If we're not happy with the end result, why would they be?

Where do you get your ingredients from?

We get about 80% of our produce directly from local farmers who we have close relationships with, and the rest comes from the local farmers' market or produce purveyors. We're lucky in LA to have some of the best produce in the world at our fingertips. When it comes to meat and fish our mission is to only use product that's sustainably raised and well-treated. We don't want to ever support organisations and farms that mistreat animals, and we spend a lot of time researching the product before it's ever brought into the restaurant. For everything else we always hunt for the best versions of ingredients available. We have lots of purveyors, sometimes just for one item.

Plenty of Wit

There's something downright 1980s about the interior of Bar Restaurant. If you happened to have lived through the neon-coloured era of scrunchies and leg warmers, you'll appreciate, even feel nostalgic in this space of dried palm fronds and giant flower arrangements atop white acrylic cubes. All of which doesn't subtract from the experimental cooking that's garnered chef Douglas Rankin a loyal following. With years working under the famed French chef Ludo Lefebvre, Rankin exhibits the fine-tuned skills of his training while also expressing his own individualism. Lamb tartare is present and paired with a kind of Lebanese-style buckwheat kibbeh, as well as mussels in Dijon cream topped with your standard serving of curly fries. For this recipe, Rankin chose to give potatoes and eggs a refined and sophisticated new life.

58

Frisée, Crispy Potato, Champagne Vinaigrette, Egg Yolk Bonito

●●●

»This is one of the first dishes that I created when we opened Bar Restaurant. It helped me answer the question of who I am as a chef and what my cuisine would be. I'm not French or Spanish but am professionally trained in both. I am a quarter Lebanese and have an affinity for all Asian cuisine. So, I took everything I loved and all my training and made something that spoke to me and my journey as a chef. A cuisine that constantly evolves through experience and culture seen through the lens of bistronomy. This dish exemplifies that ideology.«

Ingredients

Serves 2

Egg yolk bonito
1 flat of eggs (30 eggs)
1.5 lbs (700g) white granulated sugar
1.5 lbs (700g) kosher salt
10g (1 tsp) shichimi togarashi (Japanese 7 spice blend)
30g (3 cups packed) bonito

Crispy potato
2 Yukon Gold potatoes, peeled and cut in half
1 litre (4 cups) water
30g (1.20 oz) peeled garlic
25g (2 tbs) kosher salt
1/4 of a yellow onion

Champagne vinaigrette
580g (2 cups plus 2 tbs) blended oil
110g (1/2 cup) Champagne vinegar
90g (1/3 cup) Dijon mustard
65g (2.30 oz) shallots
9g (0.30 oz) garlic, peeled

Components/garnish
Potato
Cured eggs
Bonito flakes
Frisée salad, cleaned and trimmed
Champagne vinaigrette
Chive flowers (or chives if flowers not available)
Everton cheese (use Comte or a good aged white cheddar if you cannot find Everton)
Brown butter

Shopping List

[QR code]

Preparation

Crispy potato
1. In a mixer blend onion, garlic, and salt with the water until finely chopped.
2. Put potatoes in a medium saucepan and cover with the brine, ensuring potatoes are fully submerged.
3. Bring potatoes to a boil then reduce heat to low, cook for 20 minutes.
4. Drain and cool in the fridge, then place in the freezer for at least two days.

Egg yolk bonito

1. Put the salt and sugar in a food processor and blend until both are the same consistency. Remove and mix with the togarashi and bonito in a large mixing bowl. Using half the mixture line a hotel pan 5 cm/2 in deep, and make evenly spaced divots (holes) with a spoon.
2. Separate the yolks from the whites and place a yolk in each of the holes. Cover the eggs gently with the remaining salt and sugar mixture then pack down and let cure for roughly 3 weeks to a month.
3. Remove from salt mixture and rinse thoroughly. Let dry on paper towels at room temperature and store in an airtight container.
4. You may reduce the amount of eggs and adjust the ingredients accordingly.

Champagne vinaigrette

1. Put everything but the oil in a blender. Puree until smooth. Turn the speed down and slowly add the blended oil in a steady stream until emulsified.
2. Season with salt to taste.

Finishing the dish

1. Remove potatoes from the freezer and par-fry in a deep fryer or pot filled with oil at 170°C/350°F for roughly five minutes. Remove and hold on a tray lined with paper towels to soak up the oil.
2. Drop the potato back in the fryer.
3. Dress the frisée with champagne vinaigrette, black pepper, and salt.
4. Once golden brown and hot inside, remove the potato from the fryer, place back on the tray with paper towels and smash lightly with the back of a spoon. Spoon some brown butter over the smashed potato and season with fleur de sel.

Assembly

Place the potato in the centre of the plate and grate cheese all over it using a microplane. Finally, drape the dressed frisée over the top of the potato, grate the egg yolk all over the frisee using a microplane and garnish with a pinch of shaved bonito and chive flowers.

Playlist

Side dish suggestions

Buttered Jersey Royal potatoes (if the time of year is right) and perhaps a cleansing cucumber, butterhead, and lovage salad.

LOS ANGELES

Organic Harmony

Isabelle & Valentin
A jazz musician and singer who's worked in the nutrition industry, Reuss teamed up with Döring, an engineer and NGO professional, to create the organic eatery My Goodness with with a menu geared towards nutrition and wellness

Isabelle and Valentin develop their unique recipes with a strictly all-organic position, and serve their prepared dishes to Berliners on the go. Here they riff on some of favourite trends in the sector, and which surprising vegetables they include in their mix

What is the mostly underrated vegetable in Europe?

Valentin: We've got a variety of roots that are coming back into seasonal cooking. But also grains. Since the beginning we've used millet, spelt and other grains instead of the monoculture wheat.

What are the more unknown vegetables in our climate zone?

Valentin: I think it's about rediscovering what we have lost. When talking about fruit, for example, we've got the barberry that's basically as interesting or even more interesting than a goji or cranberry. We've forgotten to use the fruits and vegetables which grow around us. So grab your grandma's cookbook and just look into that. You'll have a lot of recipes that are way more appealing than what we tend to have now.

If I want to grow some ingredients in my small apartment, is that possible? How to start?

Valentin: Lots of startups are developing technologies so you can grow without actual soil in your kitchen. Most of it is directed towards herbs and little plants like tomatoes that you can grow immediately and without big preparation.

What was the most beautiful veg dish you've eaten?

Valentin: I'm a fan of simplicity. Take an artichoke and a lemon and you have a tremendously amazing dish.

What are other basic, healthy ingredients to feature in our kitchen cupboards?

Isabelle: Good fats. Such as a good quality olive oil, avocados, and nuts.

For cooking well—any general tips on process or hardware?

Valentin: Where you can, go oven-roasted rather than pan fried because you can control the heat better. Many oils turn at a certain temperature from fat into trans fats, which are dangerous and can lead to serious health problems.

Isabelle: My recommendation is to start with whole foods. You can make delicious pesto, dips and broth yourself rather than buying them in the supermarket. Especially in non-organic, traditional products there are a lot of hidden ingredients, additives, preservatives and sugar that are unnecessary and unhealthy. So start from scratch.

At a food market, how do you find the best quality?

Valentin: Buy organic and trust your sense of smell. Most vegetables that have been produced in greenhouses or brought up too fast with chemicals in the ground don't have a natural smell.

If you could invent a new type of produce, what would it be?

Valentin: A very, very sweet fruit packed with all the minerals and vitamins your body needs in one serving!

What's the benefit of organic versus non-organic?

Isabelle: It's so important to fuel our bodies with vitamins and minerals as most of us are already taking in so many toxins from our environment. That's only possible if you eat real food grown without pesticides or other harmful additives. It's also more sustainable and better for the environment.

A powerful and healthy veg-centric dish?

Isabelle: Smoothies are an easy way to get lots of vegetables and fruit in one hit.

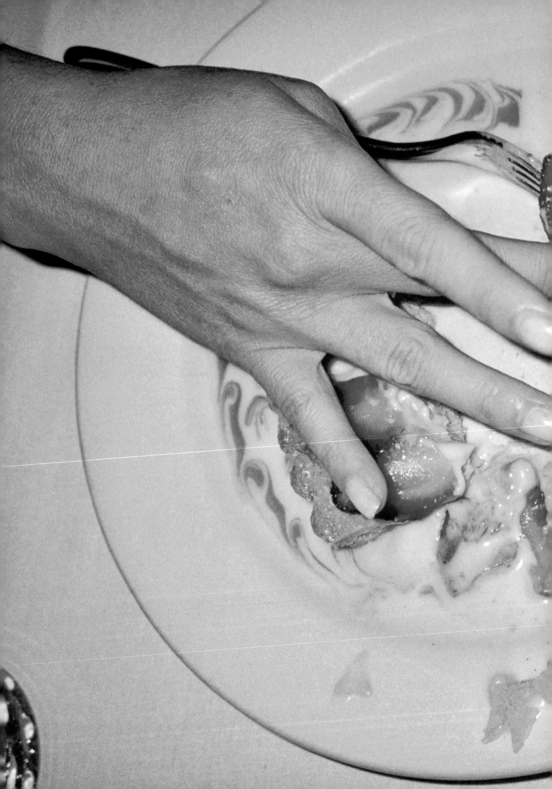

Some trips are too short for bad meals.

Make sure they're all good with the LOST iN app.

Available from LOST iN

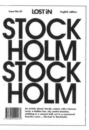

More city guides in the LOST iN mobile app

LOSTIN.COM